v v v

The Ache of the Plague

v v v

Lisa Fiedor Raines

v v v

About the Author

Lisa is from North Carolina, USA.

Her interests include: philosophy, history, international relations, politics, poetry, art, design, jazz, funk, and some good old soul.

Contents

Ruts over roots

Buried paths
Forming over years with
Sweat, love and hard work

Deformed and deforming
Conforming to a certain
Growth and depth and
Hardening over the years

Roots entwine
Crushing weight
Forcing directions and
Changing opportunities

Genetic factors
Environmental influences
Balance causes in
Personal expression

Stop "Peace for our time"

Appeasement
does not save us
from the next war

Will "spheres of influence"
bring us a bipolar world?
More stable? but never safe

A Cold War, a hot war
Will we leave it to the
"little green men"?

Is Ukraine Putin's
Czechoslovakia?
Crimea, his Sudetenland?

Hitler had no
compunctions about
breaking every pact

Does Vladimir Putin?

They fight for us!

Mothers, wives, children of Ukraine
We see you say, "Where are we?" "Where will we go?"
"We don't know anyone in Poland, or Slovakia, or Romania!"

You look up from the cold station floor
Watching as desperate people shuffle by
Following the dirty cement escape route

They don't see each other, or you, or me
The silent, cold, alone, and confused refugees
Are still one people united, Ukrainian

Husbands, sons, fathers
Sunflowers in the field
Scared, but standing strong

Willing to die for their families
To die for their neighbors
To die for their homes, lands, and country

Armed with Molotov Cocktails
A most basic weapon
Civilians face the Russian tanks

United, they fight the Russian tyrant
They fight for their democracy
For the rights of all democracies

They fight for all of us!

What war is...

Do you see the dead women
on the side of the road?
Do *you* know what war is?

Can you see the dead men,
burned and blackened?
Do you *know* what war is?

There are towns of rubble, and
cities filled with death.
Do you know *what* war is?

Where children played,
they now lay dead.

This is what war is—
it always has been.

Dollars and Sense

My, my, my, brother,
you may win when you gamble,
but you don't care about any other.

You use people in your life —
making us all into fools —
even your father and mother.

You certainly will lose
when you lie and choose
to obfuscate and cover.

Get wise, young man,
you will lose more than dollars
if you have no sense to recover.

The Genealogist

The blood making its way
Through my blue veins today
Is full of fighters and wars
And ships and shores

I wonder at the stories
Of tattered Old Glories
On each side of every
Old memo and mem'ry

It's a wonder of names
From whence we came
Of documents and titles
And pictures and Bibles

But what we use next
For historical context
Is to define us by
Yesterday and why

We leave this world
With flags unfurled
For the what, who and how
Affects more than one, now

Beware the "snip, snip" of Eugenics

From the decisions of the
American Supreme Court,

Fascism is making its way
into every one of our lives.

The Justices have declared
the States' sovereign control
over American bodies.

It has opened us up to the
horrors of forced pregnancies;

and, men, too, by losing your
bodily autonomy,

you could be subject to the
"snip, snip" of State Eugenics!

Emigrant's Song

From whence I come,
I travel back to see
My historic hosts, as
I walk in their footsteps
Hand-in-hand with ghosts

Adopted, I was, but
now that I am found
I hail from Edinburgh and Tyne
Aberdeen and Orkney
Glasgow, Mull and Skye

My people too
Have come from the East
Chased by the Valkyries
Holding for Valhalla
Berserkers in the avant-garde

From the North or South
or East or West, we have
Adopted and adapted to
New Lords and new lands
New customs and new neighbors

So I hope you understand
We all come from somewhere
Foreigners in a foreign order

Across the next boundary
Across the next border

Immigrants or invaders
It matters, your point of view
Fore-fathers and families
Leaving the motherland
As emigrants once, we grew

The Dance of the Faeries

Here is the land
where the faeries dance
In celebration of
earth and sea

Glory to the sky, and
her moon, perchance
And to the stars
we rarely see

Welcoming the sun beams
through the leaves
Infatuation is
a filtered light

Dancing in the shadows
all around us
Their reflections in
dew drops delight

Little brother, my child

Your feet are so cold,
I know what you feel.
Keep hold of hope.

As Jesus promised,
We'll see a good
Samaritan soon...

I'll hold you now;
Dry your tears.
Stay strong, my little brother.

Arizona Sunset

Red Rock altars glow
Alive in the western sun

Canyons and buttes
The backdrop of Sedona

Mountains alive with vortexes
Signified by twisted tree trunks

Touching desert trees
I feel the Earth's power

Small piles of smooth rocks
Honor the shared energy

Will you give love and stay?

Underlying power and
Movement of the waters
Nature is the course
Guiding our universe

Waves, crashing
Tumbling together
Entangled strings of
Men of war

Memories of near and far
And of who we are
Beholding our nature
What will be your future?

Do we give back
Or take a blessing
And run away
Will you give love and stay?

It's me

I so looked forward to
Your Christmas cards

Pictures of your daughter
She looked so much like you

When your Dad died
You stopped writing

Why didn't I write back
Or keep your address

I've searched for years
To tell you I love you

It's me
I miss you

Young Graduate

Think through thoroughly
Every move you make,
BEFORE you make it

Love passionately your person,
Everyone needs one

Cry when you're happy,
Laugh when you are sad

Keep things in perspective,
Especially your time
And your money

Always find the context
Of every situation

Study history, and the historian,
Art, as well as the artist

Develop an ethical code,
And live by it

Protect the people in your life

Believe deeply in what you believe

And never lose hope—
Remember,
This too shall pass

So take notes

Woke

We need more
time to focus,
to understand the
world that woke us,

the demands from those
who provoke us,
a defense from those
who choke us,

as we define
the locus of
our lives,
our times,
our rhythms,
and our rhymes.

Our lives must not be denied

If we hide, or stand aside,
we abide those who have lied
in our names, only to gain
dominance over our pain,
manifested in the pride
we have so long been denied.

We have cried, our tears have dried,
no traces could have belied
the depths and the places,
we, by our social graces,
have so rudely been denied
by language meant to deride.

We must decide how we guide
our wide-eyed children, denied
by those in power to live
and not to cower, but to give
to those on whom we relied,
are allied, and stand beside.

If the universe was created from nothing...

How is the conservation of energy possible?
According to the First Law of Thermodynamics,
energy is neither created nor destroyed.

The Big Bang theory,
the creation of something from nothing,
is patently inconsistent with this.

For conservation of energy to be correct,
the universe must be a sealed, finite system.
Is it? How do we know?

If the universe is inflating,
from what energy?
Where is it deflating?

jammin' granny - senryu

come see nana jam
bass guitar gets in your shoes
my hot granny rocks

Sweet Felicity

With ice blue hair, and
Red hot lips

Riotous acts
Of colors start

To capture her
Technique in part

But, it's the squinty laugh
That melts your heart

Sweet Felicity is
Eloquence in art

Do you know?

What I am going through?
Do you know the things that I've got to do?
What am I going through?
Do you know?

I am tired of what I have to do.
I just wish you saw the things I do for you.
What are you going through?
Do you know?

We used to laugh, now I can't talk to you.
Do you still to love me like you used to do?
What are we going through?
Do you know?

It's a mystery how to get through to you.
Is this the exit now that you will choose?
Where are we going to?
Do you know?

You know my love will see you through.
Do what you have to do.
It's time for you to choose.
Do you know?

haiku - molting

molting trees, shedding
skins of resplendent colors
spring, summer, and fall

into the freezing
white world of wonder
color brings us life

Mom's jewelry box

I used to help Mom
pick out earrings
and a necklace to
match her outfit.

I would play with
Grandma's old fancy
Art Nuevo style pins
and clip-on earrings.

Mom's taste, I think
stemmed from what we all
got her as gifts on
holidays and birthdays.

Kids can have some love
for anything gaudy,
but sometimes...
even gaudy is beautiful.

I washed your urn with my tears this

morning

I felt you here with me
I held on so tightly
All I could do is weep

It's not been four months yet
I still sob uncontrollably
I don't want to remember ...

That night in the hospital
They turned off the machines
And took you away from me

I scream, "No, come back!"
But there's no one here
All I can do is hold you now

I'm still holding your hand

Like a sledgehammer to my heart
My chest has caved in, and
I cannot breathe

They say you're gone, but
I still see the rise and fall of your breath
The nurse tells me it's the machine

Oh God, your hand is so cold, and
I can't feel your heartbeat!
This can't be happening

I knew you must go someday, but
Not like this, not this soon
I'm still holding your hand!

We like to be categorized

Archetypes
Stereotypes
Reductive persona
Am I this type or that?

Are you Red or Blue?
Independent or Green?
A Liberal or Conservative?
Black or White?
Okay, so now, why?

What religion do you observe?
Which denomination, what day?
Which house of worship do you
Populate on the holidays?
Or do you abstain?

Emotional descriptions
Pronouns and verbs
Genders free to choose
Among a beautiful spectrum
Respect in a new generation

Love is love. Agape is
Loving thy neighbor, and
The description of

God's love for us all as
The Humans' race.

The recommendations of
Jesus were to Love God, AND
Love your neighbor as yourself.
Unless you're suicidal...

Stifled Catharsis

My love, you left me bereft
I have no more tears
With which to mourn you

The ducts have dried
Just salt in my wounds
Tears somehow bleed off the pressure

I scream into a pillow
Hiding my contorted face
This is my only expression

This dry, all the more dramatic, cry
Denies me my catharsis
So badly needed, and well-deserved...

You left me.

Life's Little Rivulets

Like the Colorado river
Carved the Grand Canyon
Life's passionate rivulets
Etched Mom's every line

Years of happiness and
Disappointments eroded
Her features into soft folds
Marking her long life

We remember her when
She was young and beautiful
And as she got older
We saw her life's experiences

Beauty and wisdom
Earned over her lifetime
Marked her devotion to
God and family

He's Gone Now / The Ache of the Plague

Douse the sun and
Hide the moon
Drape all the wreaths
In black, it's too soon

No more visitors
So many more years
I feel so alone
Without you, my dear

We are the same now
You and me
You are the grace in
Everything I see

I wake up each morning
And it's still true
Guide me how to live now
I can't breathe without you

I beg you, my God
Take me home to him
My soul cries out
To be whole again

The places we went
The memories we made
They are all that matter now
The last song has played

Your pictures I've placed
All around the house
Reminding me of your smile
And why you're my spouse

The stories you told
The people you held near
Your jokes, I'll never
Remember them, I fear

So, go home, my love
God must need you now
That's the only reason
I'm still in this cold hell

I'll see you soon, though
That must be enough
The kitties still need me
Even for them it's tough

I'll look to the sky
And know that somewhere
You and I had a love
Even strangers could share

So I put down my pen
And turn off my phone
Writing today makes
Me feel so alone

A Prayer Answered

My dad died a peaceful death
He heard the Latin mass and
Celebrated it with his nurse

I know he asked with
All his belief, all his heart
And all his mind

God, please, I'm yours
In your mercy, in your Oneness
Let me be of your kindness
Please take me home

His clouded eyes
Reached for heaven
And he was gone

blank verse - a haiku

no more happy rhymes
the poem doesn't end, but
moments fade away

Your Little Hand

Roll up the sky and
Blow out the moon
No more wishes on
The first star tonight

You held our little hands
And taught us to pray
I held your little hand
And learned about forgiveness

May you know our love
Is with you, as
We know you will
Always be a part of us

We miss you, Mom

My Dad died today

Billions of people
Must choose to see
Or not to see
The death all around us

We owe it to the Earth
We owe it to our God
Life's bargain was made
Many millennia ago

Our dust must settle
Buried for an eternity
Waiting for a new world
The next one must be better

Phantom pain streams
From eyes swollen shut
Tragedy should be expected
Accepted, if not understood

Like skeletons in hollow walls

Some wounds do not heal
They fester under scars
And get buried alive

Unexpected events
Loose these mental traumas
Onto our consciousness

Abandoned memories
Like orphans re-emerging
Are quickly ushered away

Becoming skeletons
Built into hollow walls
Underpinning our fragile psyche

It's a "we" problem

Way back when, in early 2020, COVID-19 was a "them" problem.
Demonize the victim, the other, the weaker.
Exclusive, separation.

More recently, in early 2021, the virus is an "us" threat.
Will it happen to me, my friends or family?
Inclusive, but still separate from "them".

Now, COVID-19 is a "we" crisis! We all must face the immediacy!
The closeness of the disease and its variants affect us all.
We are all!
Integration, cooperation, determination, and protection.

We all live here, with and for each other.
We are all our families' keepers.
"We" are all we have.

Trumpublicans

What has happened to
the Grand Old Party?

How did Ronald Reagan's
reviled "Evil Empire"
become Donald Trump's
"Dictator's Dream Team"?

With faux outrage from
ghosts of the "Tea Party",
we have inherited a
fascination with fascism.

My way or the highway
leaves a lot of people on
the side of the road,
stranded and often forgotten,

taking too many of us
through Gullible's Travels
to the Coup of Fools
and Tools.

But our democracy did not fall

Having whipped up the contentious crowd into
a murderous mob, the soon to be former
twice-impeached president, Donald J. Trump,
unleashed the deadly weapon of armed
insurrection to assault and overtake the
Congress of the United States of America,
the legislative branch of the US government,
a co-equal branch to the Presidency.

On that cold and windy January 6th, 2021,
thousands gathered for the "Stop the Steal" rally.
The crowd jeered and cheered, celebrating
former president Donald Trump's lies about
the legitimacy of his loss in the 2020
Presidential election.

At the behest of several of the rally's speakers,
including the soon to be ex-President Trump,
thousands of loyal, "law and order" loving
Republicans, Jack-booted terrorists, and
white supremacists stormed the United States
Capitol, armed with weapons, and a noose and
gallows.

The violent and bloody traitors swarmed inside
our hallowed Capitol building, killing and
maiming loyal members of the overrun Capitol

Police. They smashed windows and broke down
doors, spread excrement on the walls, and stole
"trophies" to commemorate the riotous occasion--
which they later billed as a "friendly tour."

These anarchists attempted to destroy our
democracy, assaulting our revered republic,
breaking into the chambers of the joint session
of Congress, and interrupting the lawful
duties of government to certify the electoral
ballots of the 2020 election.

These terrorists, "good" boys, and horn-hatted
haters screamed their murderous intentions to
lynch the United States' Vice President,
Mike Pence, and Speaker of the House,
Nancy Pelosi.

But our democratic republic did not fall. It was
saved by brave men and women, risking, and
some giving, their lives to protect our democracy,
our way of life. We thank you for your sacrifice.
You will be remembered.

Falling leaves

it's September now
embrace the warmth of Autumn
and crispness of nights

October bursts with
Autumn's sweet and vivid hues
orange yellow and red

November oysters
sharing our love by the grill
giving thanks alone

lonely December
Christmas without Mom and Dad
we'll miss you so much

Real eyes realize..

the blurring lines
between life and liberty,
author and authority.

...the soft faces behind
wrinkled traces of
hate and bigotry.

...the double vision of
sowing hate and division
between people of
love and loyalty.

Real eyes realize real lies.

haiku - Christmas tears

melancholy year
saying our Christmas prayers
without Mom and Dad

haiku - Thanksgiving

November oysters
we shared love by a hot grill
giving thanks alone

Grace, Peace and Healing

Dear Creator,
Please keep our sister, Luyu Wild Dove,
in your grace, hold her in your peace,
and heal her with your divine love.
Yours always, Lisa

Educate

If we take the
Time to educate
We might even get
Rid of all the hate

Let us just pray
It's not too late
To undo our
Biggest mistakes

Let love live

No matter
What it takes...

The Deadliest Christmas

What is it worth
to be with our
beloved family,

and have them unknowingly
share the COVID-19
virus with you?

Of course, you didn't
know you were
asymptotic.

You thought it
couldn't happen
to you or our family.

Statistics and news
were just numbers
and views to you,

but now our
Dad is sick, and
Mom is alone.

You couldn't wait
a single day for
the COVID-19 test.

Exchanging gifts, and
hugs and kisses, on
the 25th of December;

going to church, and
removing your mask,

was more important
to you than our
elderly parents' lives.

Ignoring the risks
seems so foolish now.

If you had wanted
to keep our family well,
you would have stayed home.

You could have waited
for the vaccine, or
at least taken the test.

Why were you so
selfish? Why are you
so determined to be
knowingly ignorant?

I pray Mom and Dad
will still be here
for our celebrations
in this new year.

We wrest no more

We have cried,
and we have died.
Our blood is on
the American flag.

Is democracy now fleeing?
Is Lady Liberty returning to France?
Be away with your huddled masses.
We no longer yearn to be free.

As Rome's republic died,
will ours die too? The weak
Republican leader cedes power
to base radicals and extremists.

Fascist forces try to steal an election.
Armed jack-booted thugs take aim at peace.
Take our Constitution away and hide it.
We must keep it safe, lest they burn it all down.

All I have to give are tears

This cruel virus took my job,
my savings, my pride in, and
my ability to support my family.

I can't pay the rent,
the utilities, the phone bill, or
the internet connection.

The trip to the food pantry
used to be so embarrassing--
now they all know my name.

Thank goodness for the
eviction moratorium--another
month we're not homeless.

Food, gas, meds, power, and
the internet for school--
these are the highest priorities.

I'm starting to get desperate.
I look at my bills and realize
all I have to give are tears.

How is she keeping warm?

Standing in front of a store,
looking pale and cold,
she carried three bags
on her back and front.

My husband gives her
a few dollars for food.
She looks at me, smiles
and waves in thanks.

Walking away, I see her
broken gait. Her needs
are so obvious, it pulls
at my heart.

I say a prayer for her,
today, and every day.
It's cold now, and raining;
how is she keeping warm?

If all lives matter

Say his name: George Floyd
Say her name: Breonna Taylor
Say your name
if you want it to stop.

Where are we that
black people are killed
without consideration,
without pause.

Just to stay alive
when they drive
is more stressful than
you'd care to know.

Ten and two, son,
you know what to do.

Hands up!
Don't shoot!
The cry of defense,
in a desperate situation.

If all lives matter, then
Black Lives Matter!

I get no joy from this,

my lonely business trip.

The dinner was surprisingly edible.
Socializing is nice, but as you know,
I hate small talk.

At my room, I hear the sad echo
of my closing hotel door—
click, the lock confirms my loneliness.

Stale dead air swirls as
I walk through the room.
I turn on the TV for company.

This room feels so sterile
plain sheets dress a cold bed, and
pillows crackle in their sanitary cases.

I want to talk to you and decompress,
but you're three hours ahead.
I hope you're not asleep yet.

I call, but get no answer.
I'll text you. I hope we can
talk in the morning.

So far away, so out of touch,
I get no joy from
this lonely business trip.

Lies, lives, and many,

many more lives...

Where can we find an
objective truth today?

The charlatan in charge
speaks out every day,
laying bare all the cracks
in our mutual Death Valley.

This COVID criminal
battles for headlines,
while hundreds of thousands
lay dead at his feet.

The pandemic panic
is starved for air, while
the presidential power grab
claims the election was not fair.

No news is not good news,
and old news is new again.
How do we best document
these times in our lives?

News shows, newspapers,
the Web and TV,

articles, books, and
essays to read,

photos, music, and
many works of art,
give us some perspective
and a place to start.

To find the current
context though,
we must keep true
to what we know.

Original sources
we must pen,
so we don't see days
like these again.

Recovery

For weeks now
I've been quarantined,

away from you
and our family.

From our house
to a hospital,

to the ICU and
a breathing tube

helped me beat
this deadly disease,
COVID-19.

Having cleared my lungs,
I can breathe with ease,

recovery seems
possible for me.

Soon I'll be
home, happily!

Sun on my skin
is all I need.

Just One Letter

I write a letter
to my lover, C.

You know who you are;
you're everything to me.

This letter is poetry
predestined, it seems;

I think about you
endlessly.

Your lovingly written
letters I read,

convey a world
in which we could be

in love and happiness,
sensually;

Truly together,
without supremacy.

Coronavirus Courage

I see you every day,
working and worrying,
trying to keep us all safe.

Your disabilities and risk factors
put you in serious danger
every time you leave the house.

My own disabilities keep me
home-bound and isolated,
worried about you being out there,

among people who have
very little or no respect
for this virus or each other.

I see how you protect us;
I know the care you take.
Risking your health and

braving this virus,
makes me love you
all the more.

The Truth has been deregulated

The teeth have been removed

From fake news to
alternate facts

Rampant irrationality
supersedes reality

Everything is a hoax
until it is what it is

Suspend all disbelief
just to get some relief

From the attack on our grief
and the destruction of our civic belief

We met so casually

At a work meeting,
I think, if I remember
it at all correctly.

I was so shy when
you asked me to
join the group's
after work hangout.

We were fast friends, but
people saw our
intractable bond
well before we did.

One night out,
a guy at a club
asked you if he could
dance with me.
Weird!

At a separate party,
a little later that year,
you were asked if
I could come play pool
with the guys.
Really weird!

Finally, at our
favorite restaurant,
they asked us how long
we had been married!
What? It was our first
lunch date.

All of these situations
finally clued us in,
maybe we should
go out, and see
what they really mean.

My feelings grew,
overwhelming what I knew,
and you seemed to feel it, too.

That was twenty years ago.
Can you believe it!?
It's been a hard, but
beautiful, time together.

My lesson learned...
Pay attention!
Love takes time and work—
It's worth both,
If you really want it.

Devouring our power

A dour old man
Cowers behind
Flowering wreaths

Scowling he growls
About tottering
Towers and golden
Russian showers

Floundering and flailing
He fails to see
He's foundering the
Nation's economy

Deflowering our
Hallowed Constitution
He empowers fascists and
Foments racial supremacy

Glowering he dons
His snow-white cowl
Scouring any morals from
His presidential power

From Memory to Remembrance

When my memories
grow dim, and all else
fades away,
I need to feel you
close to me.

My most precious
possession is
a ringlet of your
silky brown hair.

I keep this tiny curl
in a small locket,
along with a cherished
picture of you.

I want it to stay
close to me, to be
my touchstone,
my lodestar,
my holy bones.

As I invoke this most
treasured locket, and
hold it next to
my lonely heart,

I know you'll always
be here, with me,
close enough
to touch.

A Fake $20 Bill

A man died...
Capital punishment for
A fake $20 bill?

Would you have known it,
If it were yours?

The special paper, and
Intricate patterns,
Millimeters from legit;

Should you be murdered
for not knowing your
$20 bill is illicit?

Does that make me
Somehow complicit?

Why cuffed?
Why face down, on the street?
Why murdered?

For a fake $20 bill?

Why?

Mama! Mama!

The officer was kneeling, unfeeling,
on the man's neck, as we heard him
cry out, "I can't breathe!"

With officers on his legs and back,
his handcuffed arms behind him,
he lay faced down on the street.

Bystanders gathered and pleaded
for his life, "Get off of him!," "He can't breathe!,"
"Stop! You're killing him!"

With the officer on his throat
for 9 minutes and 29 seconds,
we witnessed the horror of his murder.

"Mama!" he screamed, "Mama!"
he cried out for his dead mother,
who died two years earlier.

"Mama!" was his last word;
and the man who wanted
to "touch the world," did.

Woke?

We need more
time to focus,

to understand the
world that woke us,

demands from those
who provoke us,

defense from those
who choke us,

as we define
the locus of

our lives,
our times,
our rhythms,
and our rhymes.

We are divided

deprived,
denied, and
derided

we've derived,
described, and
decried it

this virus seems
designed for us
to die of it

My Poetry's Purpose

I'm a poet, not a pastor;
psychology, philosophy,
proliferate my proofs.

Personality, perspective,
not patronage, nor paranoia,
prove to be my persuasions.

Preachers, politicians, and
prognosticating pundits,
proliferate preposterous
propaganda, pushing
people into palpitations.

With permutations of
pacifying procrastination,
my poetry process
probes personal
potentiality, and
possibilities
for peace.

We cry blood, not tears

Our pores exude hope,
not sweat

We drink love

Writers weep war
Artists bleed rainbows

Poets spit inspiration

Politicians fart positions
Lawyers regurgitate the law

Musicians swim in beauty,
the luckiest of us all!

haiku - grey morning

clouds have descended
caught like cotton on the pines
steamy fog thickens

haiku - sunshine

heat waves shimmering
on the distant desert floor
summer's sun returns

summer's sun shimmers
on the distant desert floor
scorching everything

Anthem

Blocked by a hill,
I see the rise of
dark grey smoke.

Bright explosions
reverberate with
thunderous echoes.

Flashes of light,
red, blue, and gold,
fuel my imagination.

The smell of acrid
gunpowder wafts
on whirling winds.

A night like this,
Francis Scott Key could see
by the rockets' red glare,

enough to birth
his famous poem,
in that dawn's early light.

Little did he know
it soon would be coupled
with a bawdy tune,

and ultimately imbued
with a standard of
national import.

At the country fair

I see you,
with your far away
eyes.

Where are you looking,
for what, or is it for
whom?

Are you gazing
inward or out,
forward or back?

Do you see my
future?
Is it in fact?

haiku - stormy seaside

tempestuous waves
crash against a rocky beach
salty surf-spray stings

At the Compound

Though profound,
he confounds
with surrounding
rebounding sounds,

expounding with renown
and propounding
astounding
newfound grounds.

——-

At the compound,
we rebounded
aground, with
rounds downed,

hoping to drown
the resounding
sounds of unwound
hounds, clowns,
and crowns.

——-

Abounding with
fuel found

around our
outer boundaries,

unbound, we
went to ground,
bound to get
our bounty.

——-

We found an
unsightly mound
of unsound ground,
wound with a browned
ground cover,

encountering this,
he founded his redound
on a rewound
circle of life.

You Disappointed Me Today

You used to be happy
What happened to that?

You used to have fun
Now you have none

You used to joke and tease
Now nothing will please

You used to whistle happily
Now you treat us crappily

This is not a you
I ever wanted to see.

What is happening
to my family?

Who are you, always mad
You took away my Dad

Adoption Archaeology

These barricades are built
from each stone underneath—
overturned or unseen—
each crunch of my feet,
every stub in between.

My forts have been founded
deep within me, sealed
with a quicklime screed
of lies and deceit,
totally foreign to me.

Freud would say
I must look unconsciously,
to see what it means to me,
walled within and without
my personal archaeology.

Retired

Everything retried—
Aching on the inside
Can't even
Make it to the door

Effusive tears
Shake my many years
All that's left is fear.
Will I die here?

I miss my job
Life hurts
I sob

Every day
I remember you

Long Beach Iced Tea

Lots of shots
Gin, rummy, and vods
One of tequila, too

Triple Sec
Sour Mix
Pretty sweet with an
Acerbic wit

Oh, No cola, please
That's Long Island, see
Some Cranberry juice
Will work for me

I've Got to be
a bit Different, it seems
Preferring a Tea that's
Not a tea, and
Confusing all around me

I wrote a poem today

It made me cry.

Raw distressed emotion,
cut, as if by a knife.

Will our being heal,
remembering our life?

Please, come back to me!
Let us have no more strife!

Touched by the Flame

Sometimes it enlightens, sometimes burns...

Guiding light
Searing burn

Brilliant
Bruises

Inspired
Pain

Manic
Madness

Dynamic
Doubt

Fantastic
Fugue state

Emotions
Without

Quiet my fears, show me the lies

Please enlighten me with your wizened eyes
More mortal souls have lost their lives
On a summer's eve very like tonight

The Stench of War

The hot breath of Death hangs in the air,
smelling of seared meat and acrid gunfire;
it invites me to retch and heave.

I try to avoid sticky pools of blood;
Horrific scenes in their reflection
haunt my every dream.

These days defy credulity—
poisoning my passions, numbing my heart
to the means of this Tragedy.

We may not need
to send soldiers to bleed,
returning them home Incomplete.

The day of the bleeding
machine is at hand,
but our Victory will not seem complete.

We all must embrace
the case for Peace
to defeat the warring Conceit.

Romantic humidity

As I walk in the early morning,
steam rises from the road.
Hot summer rain hangs in the air.

A Primer in Profundity

Punditry plundering
perfunctorily purposeful
permutations of pioneering
presidential propaganda,

portending a preamble to
present potentiality, and
possible probability,

promising projections,
professing protectionism, and
preserving power,

pending problems
predicted by prescient
public protestation.

And I'm not gonna make it home

Why do I want to go home,
when you're not there anymore?

Why do I say goodbye every day,
when I wish you were here?

Why do I cry, try, dry my eyes,
deny my cries, decry my life?

Fight, flight, slight light, always right;
Lie, lie, lie, lie, lie, lie, LIE

Betrayal

I tried so hard to hold it, controlled,
but that single tear rolled silently
down my cheek, belying my true self.

Knights in White Satin

Never trying to feel
Just as our love is
We both must be real

Scary men out there
Burning the cross
Yet how will we be
Bracing for loss

Inhumanity haunts us
Robes red with reflection
Stalking each furtive kiss
Hate blinds the connection

And I love you
Oh, how I love you
Change the hearts of men
Please, God, show us how

Get out of your head

My husband said
As I tried to turn down
his volume.

Another time,
as he reminds,
I tried to change the channel.

Don't look at me
like I'm so funny,
a character on your TV!

I need you to be serious now,
wake up and
see reality!

Rainy morning - Wouldn't you know it

Cars splash through muddy potholes
and overfilled storm drains, while
hydroplaning on oily streets.

I try to avoid murky puddles,
and swift currents along sidewalks.
Always unlucky, I get drenched by both.

He is my heart

Always beating
strong and true
Living life on the inside
We're changed forever

Now, racing thoughts
Palpitations
A chilling sweat breaks
over my skin

Betrayal?
Connivance?
Why do I wonder
about faithlessness?

The night goes on
disappointment arises
Why and where, my love
I need my heart!

When does fear start?
The first midnight
or too many after?
I jump at every sound.

My heart breaks
with every slow tick

I can't help but stare
There's no solace in it

Frightened now
Wondering everything
Wreck, coma, death?
Shot? Please, god, no!

What? Dead phone?
Again? Really?
Heart, be still and strong
Please come home

Even if It's All of the Time

I want you to have
wonderful memories of us,
even if it's all of the time.

You listen to my poetry,
you look at my art,
even if it's all the time.

You have the patience
of a glacier, but I know
I'm wearing you down.

I'm sorry I do that,
all of the time,
all the time...

Love me for better,
love me for worse,
but love me all of the time.

Every day I try to do better;
every day I get a little stronger,
especially when you're with me,

all of the time.

Foolosophy

Some "Big" men
call others
"Boy", and worse.

Is it so
they can feel
like "real" men?

This must be
a fleeting
sensation!

Take Me Home

I remember when I was a child,
singing along with Dad
on long road trips home.

We would sing the oldies;
"You Are My Sunshine"
is still my favorite.

Dad loved the song,
"Take Me Home Country Road."
John Denver was so apropos.

We sang it loudly,
and often, as we rode
through the beautiful
Blue Ridge mountains.

Soon, we arrived to drive
the long country roads
to the farm, the grove,
and the small town nearby.

Now, the farm has a
highway running through it.
The house and the
barn are gone; but,

we still travel to that
pleasant little mountain town
where home and family
will surely be found.

Headphones, really?

We used to love the music
filling the house.
We sang, danced, and
joked around together.

Now we're banished to
headphones and earbuds.
You know, the kids are
awfully quiet these days.

Music's a social lubricant,
but now has become
a reason, even a cause,
for isolation.

In sharing what we hear,
and see, and feel,
we build our world,
our community, together.

Remember?

The Mourning Doves

I hear as I walk In the
early summer morning,
cooo coooo,
cooo coooo.

The telltale birdsong
proves the beautiful
grey doves have returned.

This particular morning,
three mourning doves
gathered outside
my front door.

Of what fortune,
or torture,
could this congregation
foretell?

Surely it's a sign!
I search for context,
finding only mystery.

Come, Walk with Us

If you could be perfect
Give away all your money

Give away your house
Your car, your phone

And come join us
Walk in our footsteps

Share in our all and
awe of our creator

Make the weak strong
Help the blind see

Heal the sick
Care for the wounded

House the homeless
Feed the hungry

Love the criminal
Raise the wretch

Believe in love,
for love is all we have.

The Good

Empower the oppressed,
feed the hungry,
hug the frightened,
shelter the lost.

Defend the children,
strengthen the weak,
guide the confused, and
most of all, love the lonely.

Cherish their heart with yours,
for good is in us all.

Grievous Evidence

I struggled so hard
to control it, to hold it in,
to abide the inevitable
emotional flashover.

Flushed from my eye,
down my reddened face,
the white crystals glowed,
evidence of how deeply
losing him affected me.

I wiped my face, but
my tear-smeared makeup,
ruined the facade.

Where are you now, pride?
What have you done to me?
I felt ashamed as a desperate,
grievous pain ruled the day.

Pay Attention

Just as we can never step
in the same river twice,
thank you, Heraclitus,
we can never just
rewind our lives.

We can neither pause,
nor jump it back—
no fast forwarding,
no channel guide.

There is no mute button,
nor volume control here.
If you miss something
right now,
you will never
get that moment back.

Cherish your life,
and choose wisely,
but most of all,
put the remote down,
and pay attention!

DiffAbilities

Many of us may not have
disabilities to show, but
we all have our special
abilities, you know.

To each their own,
and, beyond compare,
we live in the community,
to perceive, to share.

Bring your uniqueness,
and join us at the table.
There is no single expression
of being differently abled.

Even in ubiquity,
we have our diffabilities;
cherish them all, and
explore your possibilities.

Rhythm and Write

Please don't sound trite
Don't pick a fight
You just might be right!

Righting our wrongs
Celebrating our songs
Helps us all be strong!

We must ALL get along!
We MUST all get along!
WE must ALL get along!

If there is no law, there is no sin.

~ Romans 4:15

There is no rule that, but
by breaking it, makes it so.

Where there is a proven rule,
it is likely that therein is a custom.

Where there are customs,
what is agreed may become law.

Where there are laws,
there is regulation.

When something is regulated,
there can be licensing.

Where there is a license,
there is also a tax.

Where there is a tax,
there is a tax collector.

Where there are tax collectors,
there is often bureaucracy.

In bureaucracy, you will
likely find corruption.

Corruption breeds and
feeds upon greed.

Therein is the sin.

winter haiku

snowy wonderland
a cherry tree hibernates
cold Asian beauty

Capitalism Today

Corporate "persons"
Not paying any taxes
Laissez-faire gone wrong

Economic Definitions

Capitalism

Capital = money

Government based on money

Socialism

Social = people

Government based on people

haiku - winter

snowy wonderland
a cherry tree hibernates
wild winter beauty

Aural Infatuation

I hear my words come
Lilting out of your mouth
I need the validation

You play your saxophone
So sexy and so hot
I wish to be that instrument
you've so long sought

We make mad music
Kiss and dance up a sweat
It makes the moment hotter—
and wetter

Saxy Moment

You suckle
your saxophone
so sexy and so hot

I wish to be
that instrument
you've sought

We make
mad music, and
dance up a sweat

It makes the
moment hotter—
and wet

My Cage

Is this my crate or my cage?
Either way I'm an animal,
locked in, and wanting out

These same bars
are my protection
and my prison

Must I stay here
to stew in shame?
Will I ever get out again?

If I ever do go out again,
I hope it's for a vacation, and not the vet!

What I see in you

Love like no other
Laughter at my jokes

Hope for better days
Despair in other ways

It's been twenty years
It feels a lot longer

You're still teaching me new things
I love the excitement that brings

You bring such heart into our lives
Thank you for teaching me how to start

Between My Baby and My Boo

I love to hear you
whisper "my Boo",
especially when it's quiet,
and we're alone.

Often so formal,
"my Baby", can be
your sweet whisper,
too.

But when I see that certain
look in your eye,
I know "My Baby"
is not your only lie.

I wait to hear
which words ring true,
do you play "My Baby",
or whisper, "My Boo"?

Vincent Van Gogh, from Arles

I never knew so clearly
the acute difference
between paintings
and prints.

After collecting my
treasured prints,
the aesthetic designs
I truly enjoyed,

I drove 5 hours to
Washington, DC,
to see the inspired
treasures from his
brother's collection.

——-

Vincent's thick paint sparkles,
unexpectedly, beckoning me
to see the miracle inside
of a heavy golden frame.

His aggressive strokes
of vibrant color
push me away,
making me back up
to see it all.

In looking at the structure,
I never expected to
see the 3D reality.

This sensual and sensational
bump map gives me
a detailed exploration of
the curves and valleys of
the French countryside.

Capturing the night sky,
his every star glows, shining,
flowing on a swirling
river of darkness.

So artfully laid on
a giant canvas,
I move closer to see
his handiwork.
A guard moves me away.

The glowing, sparkling
night scenes of an Arles cafe
invite me to see,
through his eyes,
the place he spent
so many nights.

————

I left DC with
many more prints
in hand, pictures
I wanted as
reminders of his
miraculous works.

I still remember
vividly, my lovely,
albeit rainy,
long weekend
in Washington, DC.

Sheltering Angel

I feel protected
within your unearthed grotto,
carved of root and bough.

My dear guardian
how long had you lived within
the roots of this tree?

What force befell your
enormous trunk and broke your
boughs and broad branches?

What set you free from
your arboreal prison,
allowing us to shelter

within your well-worn wings?
As you expose your visage to us,
we are blessed to see your face.

Young girl, I remember you

Dressed up and dying
For attention
For love
For family
For identity

So needy,
Please see me
Please love me
Please help me
Please show me the way

Must I die first?
Will you know me?
Will you mourn me?
Will you bury me?

Please, just remember me

Memes of the mind

Reality
Defines itself
As it is revealed

Revelations
Become
Real

More than truth,
They become
Dreams & shadows

Memes of the mind

Selfish Peace

She'd shed a tear,
tearing herself away,
a way to find her selfish peace,
waiting for the weight to be lifted away.

For each one of us, apiece,
we must find a way to weigh,
to piece together our piecemeal ways,
waiting for the way to our selfish peace.

swelter in place

claustrophobic air
southern summer's humid heat
too steamy to breathe

Institutional Slavery

In the prison-industrial complex
corporate prisons extort
the labor of prisoners

There is no hope of freedom
from these "corrective"
labor camps

Slaves dressed up as prisoners
yearn for the promised land of
liberty and justice for all

Can Cats Be Trained?

Let's see: Spot, come here!

Buttons, buttons, buttons

Circles, circles,
circles in circles
strewn up and down
slippery stairs

I wind around,
round and around,
up and down
to this tiny turret now

The mouse king
hoards buttons, you see,
buttons, buttons and
many more buttons

These are the gem stones
of the tiny world around us,
found and treasured
like little jewels.

Looking for General Winter

Oh, no, my dearest prince!
Who turned you into this
beautiful Sussex rooster?

I must venture into
the vast Russian countryside
to search for help.

I hope General Winter can help me
find the cruel wizard that
bewitched you so.

You must stay warm
in the farmhouse now.
Avoid anyone with a cleaver!

Great Expectations, Redux

As I wear my veil,
I remember him.

I waited at the altar.
What happened?

My hair is still dressed
with curls and flowers.

But my made-up facade
is cracking and peeling.

How do these lilies
stay fresh?

Pip, I hope you learn what
devastation feels like.

Warning!

The Implication
of the Community
Coalition
Grows beyond
the Imperial
Expectation

Octogenarians

Dear Mom & Dad
We're so blessed
to have you
around!

Dad, you still drive
Mom, you still ride
I know you both have
God at your side

I worry, too
about the both of you
Don't ever think
I'm not here for you

I put my number in
your phone
Use it daily, and
you'll never be alone

haiku - summer air

steamy summer rain
humidity everywhere
feels too thick to breathe

The Rose Window

Through the heavy haze,
I see the sun's rays,
streaming into
the cathedral.

Having pierced the
deeply colored
stained glass rose,

the ray's rich colors
reveal the intricate
patterns on the floor
in front of me.

I behold beauty in the air, and
feel God's warmth upon us,
in our cathedral,
Notre-Dame de Paris.

The Drama Inside

Colors and shapes
writhe under his skin
trying to escape

The painter's deft
brush strokes master
his roiling psyche

Tension and release
are captured inside the mask
showing his inner life in stark relief

haiku - ash rises

each layer burns off
lifted by a quick whisper
light grey ash rises

Maybe that's why..

A kiss a day keeps
the lawyers away.

Why does a w look
like a double v,
not a double u?

Why do the idle rich obsess
over the idle poor?

Kids' days are a bigger proportion
of their lives than adult days;
maybe that's why it takes so long
to grow up.

The Birth of Creativity

From a simple source
We receive our DNA

From an egg and seed
Fertilized with all we need

As one cell becomes two
Two cells become four

We become an exponential
Leaf on our family tree

Once born we can see
How the mix of time and genes

Education, motivation, and
Many other means

We will manifest in our creativity, and
Help determine our identity

Reflections on how old we seem

My memory of myself and
the reflection I see

Are as incongruous as
what I might perceive.

As I reflect about
what this means to me,

I try to do so creatively.

Some seem to stay
the way they used to be,

Telltale signs of clothes, or hair,
or needing a shopping spree.

These things can help us see
where they are in their reality.

Do they feel 50 or 23?
Take a close look and

You might see the age or
youth they wish to be.

Nagging bird

Caw caws, cawing
cacophonous caws!

Calls like nails
on a chalkboard,

constantly cawing
to me, "Nevermore."

Stop! Away with your
constant caws,

causing confusion,
causing alarm.

Please do not caw to me—
Stay away, forevermore!

A Bee's Day

Golden honeybee
I see your destiny

Flitting from tree to tree
Finding nectar for honey

Returning home to see
How fruitful your bounty will be

As the long sunset colors stream
Across the sky: red, gold, and green

Denying Darwinism today

Seems to me, irrationality believed.
To exclude teaching scientific biology,
A theory about our world,, about what we see,
due to theology, is a failing ideology.

By studying evolutionary means,
humanity can be seen as one of many
species that came to be, originally,
out of the primordial sea.

To breathe with you

The nurses open the curtains,
but all I can see is glare.

From what I can tell, it's been
weeks of grey and cloudy skies.

I seem to sleep a lot, and
each day goes by without emphasis.

Everyone I see is masked, shielded,
and wrapped like a mummy.

Checking this, poking that,
I haven't even learned names yet.

Beeping machines, drips and tubes
Snake in and across my body,

seeming to writhe on the floor--
in my delirium, I hope!

I've not had any visitors, and
miss you all so much.

The hope of coming home is
my only motivation.

To breathe in life with you,
to hold you in my arms again,

These are the reasons
to keep opening my eyes,

pleading, hoping, crying,
I want to go home.

Political Definitions

It's important that
we all know the language and
context of the words
we hear, see, and use.

It's essential if and when
you are having that (ill advised)
political discussion over
the holiday dinner table.

Democracy
Demos = people
Government by the people

Republic
Public = community
Government by elected individuals representing the citizen body

Dictatorship
Dictate = speak
Government by a political leader who speaks with absolute power

Libertarianism
Liber = free
Government based on liberty, especially with regard to thought or
conduct

Liberalism

Liber = free, open

Government based on guarantees of individual rights and civil liberties

Conservatism

Conserve = preserve

Government based on preserving what is established, and limiting change

Authoritarianism

Authority = control

Government based on centralized power and limited political freedoms

Fascism

Fascio = group

Government based on exalting nation, and often race, above the individual, with autocratic power, and a dictatorial leader

Totalitarianism

Total = complete

Government based on centralized control by one person with absolute power

Who is She?

For me, the "She" is...
my domineering superego,

drowning out my id, and
suppressing my fragile ego;

nagging, and critical,
distrusting, and doubtful,

attacking my memories with
"shoulda, woulda, coulda" thoughts.

Why I "shoulda" done better,
What if I "woulda" followed through,

How I "coulda" done more,
When I need to let it all go.

Refreshing my View

I open my browser,
and what do I see,
a tiny little "2"
right next to me.

A few more likes,
I thought there would be.
Can you please leave a
comment to read?

I add my thoughts
to this list and that,
shopping my
ideas around.

It's disappointing to me
when I refresh and see
a "o" where I was hoping
there'd be "3."

haiku-bull moose

leaning on a tree
a bull moose scratches his back
leaves fall around him

haiku - beautiful masquerade

golden moon rising
stunning water shines
on your curls

silver orbs above
are jealous of your twinkling eyes
hinting at your beauty

for you my love, a bloom
reveal your secret identity
share your lovely face

Winter's Rest

brings out the best of springtime

The depressing cold,
suppressing , repressing

Takes hold of the sun's
warm caress

Shows off springtime's
golden dress

Although we've never met

I hear your voice
through your
music and poetry.

You stir
my memories
with your

syncopated
rhythms and
lyrical melodies.

I feel these in your
songs, and they
stay deep inside me.

I wonder
where you are,
what you see;

what gives you
such inspiration for
your sonorous beauty.

I listen again,
and again I feel
you take me.

Will I ever meet you,
or will I find you
in another reality?

In the tapestry of yesterday and tomorrow

Evolution is revolution,
in its own way.

Our writings, songs, and works of art,
give context to today, and a frame of reference
for tomorrow's evolution.

When the library at Alexandria was set aflame,
we lost untold books of history, art, philosophy,
medicine, mathematics and more.

We not only lost these precious works,
we lost context for studying the past—
unmooring our subsequent evolution.

Each lyric, melody, and piece of art
is affixed in time—documenting the present
and influencing the future.

This poem is simply another perspective,
another strand, in the tapestry of
yesterday and tomorrow.

The Ultimate Indoor Picnic

Scones with clotted cream and strawberry jam
Small cucumber and smoked salmon sandwiches
Wonderfully rich tea cakes and sweet macarons

Lovely little cups and dainty tableware
A formal tea with His Lordship, Earl Grey
A truly great treat for an American guest

Charity is a gift from love

Love does not have to be earned
Love is to be shared

Trust should not be assumed
Trust can only be built

Respect cannot be commanded
Respect is to be given

Happiness cannot be purchased
Happiness comes with mindfulness

Peace must not be imposed
Peace can only be found with humility

Faith cannot be pessimistic
Faith is always hopeful

Charity must not be coerced
Charity is a gift from love

My fire angels

Keep warm my little children.
I can feel your heat in my heart.
I will bring you out of
the fire soon.

I am still and
feel your heartbeats.
You three are literally
a part of me now.

I vow to protect you
as you will protect me.
We come from fire, and
it is fire we will use

for good, for freedom,
for protection of the weak,
the slave, the newly unbound,
and the unsullied.

A little time helps to lengthen the

perspective

It's been seven months now
November will be our eleventh anniversary

I remember the promises we made
We were to head to the Blue Ridge mountains

I'll sprinkle your ashes in the little pond
Out by the gazebo nearest the Blowing Rock

I'll stay at the lovely winery in Banner Elk
Where we got married and spent our honeymoon

I'll have brunch at the village cafe, and
Drive along the Blue Ridge Parkway

I may not able to walk much now, but
I must try to make it there for us

You keep me strong, my love, so
I won't be going alone

Heart Failure is Not a Failure of Heart

We may be old and tired, and
Our bodies may be broken down, but
Our heart has not failed

If we cannot make it to
The front lines, we will
Hold the line at home

Our diversity is our strength, and
We can be the nation we believe in
We must not lose our faith in Spirit

The silence is so loud

I can't hear you
over the silence

It's a deafening
suppressant

For how many years
have I had you in my head

Always there loving
and coaching me

Now that you're gone
your voice is too soft

Memories fade and
the silence is so loud

Do you know?

What I am going through?
Do you know the things that I've got to do?
What am I going through?
Do you know?

I am tired of what I have to do.
I just wish you saw the things I do for you.
What are you going through?
Do you know?

We used to laugh, now I can't talk to you.
Do you still to love me like you used to do?
What are we going through?
Do you know?

It's a mystery how to get through to you.
Is this the exit now that you will choose?
Where are we going to?
Do you know?

You know my love will see you through.
Do what you have to do.
It's time for you to choose.
Do you know?